A Chil

When Someone Dies

101 ways to help you cope

Bill Merrington

with illustrations by
Melody-Anne Lee

kevin mayhew

kevin mayhew

First published in Great Britain in 2008 by Kevin Mayhew Ltd
Buxhall, Stowmarket, Suffolk IP14 3BW
Tel: +44 (0) 1449 737978 Fax: +44 (0) 1449 737834
E-mail: info@kevinmayhewltd.com

www.kevinmayhew.com

9 8 7 6 5 4 3 2 1 0

ISBN 978 1 84867 106 5
Catalogue No. 1501144

Illustrations and design by Melody-Anne Lee
Edited by Linda Ottewell

Printed and bound in Great Britain

About the author

Bill Merrington has been an Anglican priest for 25 years. Originally an analytical chemist, after a serious illness he retrained in ministry and has since led churches in city, town and countryside in the West Midlands. Bill has a PhD in Psychology specialising in the understanding of the long-term impact in parents when a child dies. He has carried out research in Britain, Lebanon and Africa, looking at the cross-cultural impact of death. He has spoken at a number of national and international conferences and lectures regularly at universities. Bill has written a number of books for both adults and children. He is currently the Lead Chaplain at Bournemouth University and runs Counselling Care, a support organisation for bereaved parents and children.

Bill is married with three grown-up children.

For my children,
who have taught me so much about playing,
laughing, crying and not taking life too seriously.

A word about this book

When someone close to you dies, it's like starting a journey, one you have never travelled before. In this book we will think of it like a bicycle ride. Sometimes there are no road signs, the road gets bumpy, the wind and rain blow at you and you seem to be all alone. At other times the sun is shining, you are enjoying the ride and have friends around to support you. The journey seems short but it often turns out to be longer than you think. This book is to help you on your journey. Others have travelled this way before and some of their wisdom is in this book to help you. You might want to read it from beginning to end but you can also dip into it and just read a particular page when you feel like it. So, let the journey begin.

As you read this book and perhaps do the exercises, remember that:

- you can ask for help at any time
- sometimes you end up with more questions than answers
- you can keep reading the same page over and over
- it's ok to cry
- you are a unique, special person and you will react to your loss in your own special way.

While reading this book it will help to have a notebook or diary by your bed and a special box (a shoebox is ideal) in your bedroom for anything you write or make.

1
Riding a bike

When you get your first bicycle, before you start riding, you find yourself first learning all about the bike: tyres, saddle, pump and bell. It's the same when someone dies. There are new words you haven't heard before. Here are three words you might hear:

The **bereaved** are people who have had someone close to them die. Everyone at sometime in their life is bereaved.

Grief is how you feel inside of you when someone dies. You don't look any different but you might feel all strange inside.

Mourning is what people do when someone dies. People who are mourning go to funerals and sometimes they easily get upset, angry or cry. In the past, people would dress in black to show that they were in mourning. But today you can't tell if a person is mourning because they mostly act and dress normally.

Are you bereaved? Have you had strange feelings inside? Have you behaved differently since the death of someone?

2
Keep a diary

When you are not thinking clearly, everything can become a muddle. When someone dies, it can be hard to picture them. Even though we might think about them all the time, we can struggle to remember their face. If you break a leg or an arm you would get a plaster cast put on it that would be seen by everyone. But when the mind isn't working properly, no one can see or recognise it. It means that it becomes easy to forget memories and thoughts. We can have lots of questions shooting through our head, only to then forget them when we want to ask someone.

We need to help our mind recover from the shock of someone's death. One way is to keep a diary of ideas, thoughts, prayers, questions, drawings and doodles. In this way we don't have to hold on to these things but we can put them safely in the book to look at another time. As the weeks and months go by, you can look back and see how far you have travelled.

Keep a diary or notebook with a pen by your bed.

3
Stabilizers

When you have never ridden a bike before, you just can't get your balance. As soon as you get on the bike you fall over. It's very hard to pedal, steer and keep your balance. That's why you need stabilizers to steady the bike or someone to run alongside you to help you keep your balance.

It's like this when you are bereaved. You have never felt like this before. Home, school, friends and family all seem different. Often, the people closest to you have also lost their balance and feel strange. That's why when someone close to us dies, we need people around us to support us.

Imagine you are on a trampoline, being thrown up and down. Who would you want to be standing by the side ready to catch you? Draw a picture and include those who will support you.

4
Elastic band

When adults wearing long trousers ride bikes, they often tie up their trouser bottoms with an elastic band. This keeps the trousers clean from the oil on the chain. Imagine you had an elastic band tied between you and the person who has died. When he or she was alive, the elastic band kept you close to each other. When you were apart, the elastic band stretched and made you feel uncomfortable because you missed the person. But now they have died it's as if the elastic band has snapped.

Three things occur when this happens. First, when the band snaps, it twangs back at you and it hurts. Secondly, you want to fix the band and get the person back. Thirdly, you try and make sense of what has happened to you. This is the journey you are now on. You feel hurt inside at the death of your special person. You want to get them back, but can't. And so you have lots of questions to try and make sense of what's happening.

Can you remember when your special person went away for a short time? What was it like? How did you feel when they came home? Can you write a story about it?

5
Road-map

Whenever you go on a journey, you need a map to guide you. A map shows you where you have been; it reminds you of special places and memories. It also helps you to see exactly where you are at this moment. You can also use the map to see where you want to go and how to get to your destination.

On a piece of paper, make a map of where you live. On it, include places you have been with your special person. It might include holidays or special events like Christmas and birthdays that you remember. It might include things you did with your special person, like swimming or going to the park or playing a game at home. On the map include events from the past few weeks. This might include visiting your special person ill at home or in hospital, or going to the funeral. Then on the map draw things you would like to happen in the future. Perhaps where you would like to go or things you would like to do.

Why not show your map to someone you trust and then keep it safe in a special place?

6
A punctured tyre

Sometimes you are riding your bike and suddenly you get a punctured tyre. It's unexpected and it can leave you feeling very upset. You might feel like throwing your bike down and crying.

If you have a pump, you might try and re-inflate the tyre. But the more you pump, the more the air escapes and the tyre remains deflated. There is nothing else to do. You don't feel like pushing your bike home, so you sit down on the path and cry. When you are finally ready, you have to pick the bike up and head home. Somehow the crying gives you the energy to move on.

This is how it feels when someone close to you dies. You can't fix it. You can't get them back and no one seems to understand how you feel. Most people cry a lot when someone dies. It's ok to cry and it may help you to feel a little better. Eventually you have to get back to school, play, meet friends and do all the things you used to do. But for now it's ok to give time to crying.

Draw cartoon-strip pictures of you on a bike journey, getting a puncture. Finish the pictures with you getting home safely.

7
Jigsaw pieces

Have you ever done a jigsaw? You can spend hours looking for the right piece. First the corners, then the sides and finally you fill in the middle. But it's so easy to bump the table and knock the whole jigsaw onto the floor. Pieces go everywhere. Very slowly you have to find the pieces, turn them over the right way and start to make sense of it all. Sometimes you keep trying the same piece into the same space but it just doesn't fit.

When a person dies, it can leave you feeling just like the jigsaw might. It's very hard to make sense of what has happened. You may have many questions to ask. Some questions your nearest relatives can answer. A school teacher or headteacher can help with some but you might also want to ask the doctor or nurse a question.

Just like the jigsaw piece that doesn't fit, we might not be happy with the answers we get. We may need to ask the same question more than once. Sometimes three or four times until we are content with the answers we get.

As we find the answers we can begin to make sense of what has happened to us.

Why not have a go at doing a favourite jigsaw? As you do so, think about the questions you might have. If it helps, write them down so that you can ask someone when you are ready.

8
A missing jigsaw piece

When you pick up all the jigsaw pieces off the floor, you don't always realise that there might be some missing. It's only when you have nearly finished the picture that you notice one or two pieces are not there. This is very annoying and although you look all over the room, you might not find the missing piece. But at least by now you can make sense of the picture.

There may be a question about the person who has died that people can't answer. Just like when we have a missing jigsaw piece, this is not a nice feeling. But slowly, over time, we begin to build up a picture of understanding what has happened. Sometimes there just aren't clear answers to our questions. But we shouldn't stop searching for answers. As you get older you might find new answers that will give you a better understanding.

Why not write down or draw the questions you have and the answers that are given? Keep them safe and then at a later time you might like to see if you want to re-answer the questions.

9
Help, I've fallen off my bike

Have you ever fallen off your bike and hurt yourself? Perhaps you've scraped your hands or made your knee bleed. You can be too upset to know what to do. This is when we need a friendly adult to help us clean the wound and bandage up the hand or leg. Sometimes we will see a doctor to check that everything is ok.

When someone close to you has died, you can feel as if you have just fallen off your bike. You feel hurt even though there are no scratch marks on your body. That's not to say you don't have aches and pains. Some people get headaches, others find sleeping difficult. These aches and pains are not serious and it's very normal to feel like this. But it can be good to see a doctor to talk about them and to be reassured.

Can you draw your body and colour in where your aches and pains might be? If you go to the doctor with a family member, take the picture with you.

10
Friends who help

Do you ever find yourself playing with one friend one day but another day deciding to play with someone else? You can spend all day with friends from school but then go home and play with brothers, sisters or friends in the street. Sometimes you might enjoy cycling with others but there is also a time to enjoy your bike by yourself. There are also times when you might not want to spend time with a particular person and that's ok.

When someone special dies, we need to decide who we want to spend our time with. Some people are very helpful and supportive while others are not so helpful. And sometimes we just want to be left on our own. It's ok to choose what you want.

Draw a small circle and write your name in the middle. Then draw bigger circles around the first one. In one circle write down the name of your closest friend or relative. Gradually add all the people who are special to you, those closest to you near the centre and those less close in the outer circles. It's good to be reminded of all the people who will support you.

11
Cloudy days

Do you like sunny days that are warm and you can play outside all day, or rainy days when you can jump in puddles and keep cosy in the house? We all like different types of days but we don't have any control over the weather. We have to adjust what we wear and what we do according to what is happening outside. Some days we can ride our bikes and other days we have to leave them safe inside. We all have good and sad days, regardless of the weather. But when someone is bereaved, at first they can have more sad days.

When you wake up in the morning with your curtains drawn, you don't know what the weather is like. It's like that when you are bereaved. Some mornings you wake up and you feel fine and happy to go to school. On other days you can feel very sad, angry or upset. We still have to get on with daily things like getting dressed, having breakfast and going to school. But we have to be a little kinder to ourselves when we are having sad days.

Make four pictures of yourself, one looking sad, another smiling, the third looking sad and smiling and the fourth with a question mark. When you are having a sad or good day, stick a picture on your bedroom door to let others know how you are feeling. Sometimes we have a day full of mixed feelings, or we just don't know how we are feeling, so use the picture that fits you for that day.

12
Sleep

When you have been out playing on your bike or with friends all day, you can be really tired and it's easy to fall asleep. But when you are thinking a lot about what has happened in your family, it can be difficult to fall asleep at night. The body is tired but the mind is busy thinking and trying to make sense of what has happened. If you can't sleep, see if these ideas help:

– *Try not to sleep in the daytime as this spoils your sleep at night.*
– *Make sure you have had some exercise in the daytime with plenty of fresh air.*
– *Try not to play computer games just before you go to bed.*
– *Read a book in bed.*
– *If you are thinking about the dead person, talk to them quietly and let them know how you are feeling. Tell them about your day. We don't know if they will hear but it will help you.*
– *Say a prayer to God about the dead person and yourself.*
– *If you have questions in your mind, write them down in a book or diary so that they are safe and you don't have to keep thinking about them.*

13
Dreams

Some days we can feel like a boat bobbing up and down on the sea, tossed to and fro by the waves. At times there seems to be no horizon ahead and we are unclear about where we are going. When a loved one has died, we can find ourselves dreaming a lot. Dreams are like the world that lies below the surface of the water. They can represent the things we haven't had time to think about during the day.

Sometimes we dream about the person who has died. They can be very real to us in our dreams. Often we don't remember our dreams when we wake up, at other times we can remember them clearly. Some dreams are special and make us feel good. But we might also have dreams that make us feel sad or negative. Eventually dreams about the dead person stop and we begin to dream about other things in our life.

Remember, dreams are not real. Even when they feel real, they are just dreams.

- *If you have special dreams that you remember, write them down as soon as you wake up.*
- *If you have a negative or scary dream, try drawing it and then add something or someone big and special to the picture to eat up or destroy whatever it is in the picture that frightens you.*
- *Telling a special friend about your dream can help.*

14
First-aid kit

When you fall off your bike and hurt yourself, an adult will often turn to the first-aid kit in the house to find some ointment, plasters or a bandage to make you better. We have a first-aid kit to care for us when we hurt ourselves physically. When we are upset because of the death of a special person, we are not hurt physically but we still feel hurt inside us.

We still need a first-aid kit but it has different things in the box. It might contain a toy to comfort us, a special song that we like, a special memory of the dead person, a favourite food or drink we like, a special story-book or poem, something we enjoy doing (like going for a walk, or playing on the swings), or a special friend or relative that we know will help us.

We can't put all of these things in a box, but we can remind ourselves that we have all of these things to help us.

Divide a piece of paper in half. On one side draw out what goes into a physical first-aid kit. On the other side draw out what is in your special first-aid kit to help you. When you are feeling sad and don't know what to do, look at your special list and choose something to comfort you.

15
Breakfast

When you wake up in the morning, whether you feel good or sad or just sleepy, you still need energy for the day ahead. Breakfast is like the first gear on a bike. It gets us started for the rest of the day. If we miss it, then it's like riding a bike in the highest gear. It becomes really hard to get going and we soon get tired during the day.

Your family and the person who has died would want you to have a good day ahead of you. By having breakfast you are not only helping yourself, but also those who love you not to worry about you. Sometimes we are angry with the dead person or our relatives and might refuse to eat breakfast to spite them. But there are much better ways of dealing with our anger (see **Anger**, page 48).

Get permission to take your breakfast to a favourite place in the house so that it becomes a treat. If it's summer try and have your breakfast outside in the garden.

16
Eat colourful food

When we are feeling low, it's very natural to lose our appetite and not want to eat much. But if we don't eat well, then it affects our physical body, which then affects how we feel inside. Sometimes we just have to eat well, whether we feel like it or not. It's a bit like going to school. It's something you just have to do whether you want to or not. Why not ask the cook of the family if you can help to prepare the meal? Make your meals into a game: see how many different-coloured foods you can eat. Invite a friend to your house. When you are busy chatting, eating food becomes less hard work.

Make a list of your favourite foods and see if your relative can get them.

17
Fresh air

Have you ever been asked to paint a picture and not known where to start or had your computer freeze and just not work? When someone special dies we can feel the same way. We don't know how to react or what to think or do. It's a new experience that we have never encountered before, so it's understandable.

Many people who have been in this situation have found that going for walks and getting plenty of fresh air helps both the body and the mind. Sometimes you might find that during a walk your mind is blank and you don't think anything. At other times you might find you are thinking about many things. That's ok, you don't have to work everything out all at once and at least you are helping your physical body, which will in turn help how you feel inside.

Have you got a favourite walk, perhaps with special memories? Ask a friend or relative to go with you.

18
Keep active

Keeping active is sometimes the last thing we want to do when we are not feeling well. But swimming, running, walking or riding your bike is a good way of helping the body to release some of the pain within. Exercise also increases our confidence and gives us the energy for the tasks ahead. It can also give us a break from thinking or talking.

This activity doesn't have to be for very long. Begin by doing just a small amount every day. Gradually you will find that it will help you feel stronger. Find a friend to do a sport you like. Although you may not feel like doing it, by making the effort, it will help you. One day you will look back and be glad you kept going.

Why not get your bike out and give it a good clean?

19
How do you eat an elephant?

How do you eat an elephant? The answer is simple, a bit at a time. Not that anyone wants to eat an elephant. But sometimes we feel we have things to do that seem really big, like an elephant and we just don't know how to tackle them. Things which we used to find easy to do can now seem hard work after someone has died. Going to school, concentrating in class, doing our homework or even doing an activity that we loved, can now seem very difficult.

This is because our mind is thinking about the person who has died and what has happened to us. This is very normal and eventually our energy and enthusiasm will return. But it will be slow at first. We have to give ourselves time to adjust. So be kind to yourself and do things in shorter bursts. If you find school difficult, then get a relative to speak to the teacher about making things a little easier for you. Bit by bit you will find yourself able to do more things.

Can you write or draw a list of the things you now find difficult?

20
A pack of playing cards

In a pack of playing cards there are 52 individual cards. Each one is unique with its own picture and special colour. Have you ever tried to shuffle them? It's so easy to drop them on the floor. When you are bereaved it can feel as if you are holding all of the cards in your hands. Only on each one is not a picture but a question. There are just so many questions when someone dies.

Sometimes the questions come all at once and we can hardly hold on to them. At other times we can have one question stuck in our mind, going round and round. Then we find we forget the very question we wanted to ask. All of this is very normal. What can help is to write the question down when you think of it. Keep the questions safe because you might not be able to get all the answers straight away. Not everyone can answer your specific questions, some can't be answered and others will be answered at a later time.

Why not write the questions in your diary or notebook or make your own playing cards? Put pictures on one side and a question on the other.

21
It's good to talk

If someone breaks a leg they get a plaster cast to wear for weeks and weeks. Everyone knows they have a broken leg because it's hard to hide a cast. Some people allow their friends to draw and write on the cast. But when you are bereaved, although people might at first know, they can soon forget. People don't know what to say or whether to mention the name of the person who has died. This can mean that you feel no one is interested in you or cares.

You can find you have no one to talk to. Sometimes this is ok as you might not want to talk. But when you are thinking often about the dead person and what has happened to you, most people find it helpful to have someone to talk to. It might mean talking about your special person, the things you did or said together, special memories, times when you laughed and times of sadness and difficulty. It's good to talk and it can make you feel better inside.

Have you got someone you can talk to? It might be a relative, teacher or friend. If not, then ask your head teacher who might help you find someone.

22
A time to laugh and a time to cry

Can you think of a time when you couldn't stop *laughing?* With tears rolling down your face, it's hard to keep your body still with such laughter. What was it that made you laugh so much?

Can you also think of a time when you couldn't stop *crying?* Perhaps hiding your face in your hands and catching the tears. It's good to laugh and to cry. The tears help to get rid of all the feelings inside us. Even though someone close to you has died, it doesn't mean you can't still remember them with laughter. Think of the special times you might have had with them and share the story with someone.

When we cry after someone has died, it's a sign that we must have loved them. So don't fight back the tears, let them flow.

Ask your relatives about a time when they couldn't stop laughing.

23
Fizzy drinks

Have you ever taken a can of fizzy drink with you on your bike? When you come to open it, the gas gushes out and splashes you all over. But if you open the can slowly and gently and let the gas out gradually, then you don't get so wet. Our bodies are like that can of pop. When we get shaken up by the death of someone, we can fill up with all sorts of feelings, just like the gas in the can.

There are feelings of sadness, anger, helplessness, being afraid, confused, worried, frustrated, ashamed, numb, jealous, gloomy, embarrassed, guilty, fearful, searching, and more besides.

If we don't let those feelings out slowly, they can spill out suddenly and we can find ourselves getting angry or upset with people around us. We'll talk about these feelings later in the book.

Can you draw a fizzy-drink can and think of a name for it? Design the label. What would be in your can of feelings?

24
A special place

Do you have a special place where you feel safe and cosy? It might be somewhere outside in your garden or in the park. Perhaps a tree house or den or it might be in the house, in your bedroom. We all need special places where we can just be by ourselves.

Find a favourite place that is quiet to sit by yourself. Breathe slowly and deeply. Tense each part of your body and then relax it. Start from the head, then the shoulders, the arms, hands, legs and toes. Continue to breathe slowly and deeply. As you relax your body, now relax your mind. Picture a special place, somewhere that you have fond memories of. Remember the shapes and colours of the place. Remember why it's a special place for you. Now when you are ready to leave your special place, do the physical exercise again by tensing and relaxing the body. Open your eyes and remind yourself of where you are sitting.

25
No one understands

It's easy to think that no one understands just how you are feeling. After all, you are unique and although many people have had a relative or friend die, their story is not the same as yours.

Sometimes relatives don't talk to you because they don't want to upset you, while friends can say the wrong thing and upset you. And the very time you want someone to talk to you, they don't. Sometimes we just don't know what we want; to be by ourselves, to talk to someone or have someone talk to us. No wonder it's confusing for everyone.

So try and forgive those who upset you, give some slack to family and friends, and be kind to yourself because one day someone will need your help.

Write in your notebook
the things people say
that annoy you.

26
What to say

One of the big fears adults and children have is what to say when other people ask you questions.

You might get asked: How are you? What does it feel like? Why did the person die? Did you go to the funeral?

We don't really know what people will ask us but we can help ourselves by thinking through a few answers beforehand. There are no right or wrong answers, just ones that you are comfortable with.

In your notebook write down the questions you have already been asked. Are there any other questions you are worried about? Get someone to help you find the answers you are happy to use.

27
Playing is good for you

Have you been on a see-saw lately? It goes up and down constantly. You might feel like this at times. Sometimes you want to play and be out with your friends and at other times you just want to sit and do nothing. Your friends might not understand why you keep changing, but that's just how it is for bereaved people.

Even when you are feeling low, there are some things that are good for you. Drawing, painting, helping someone to cook, gardening, or just doing your normal play things will all help you slowly to feel better. At first you don't have to do something for very long, just give it a go.

What do you enjoy doing the most?

28
Be prepared

When boy scouts and girl guides go camping they have a saying which is, 'Be prepared'. This means that they have to be ready for what might happen when they are in the countryside in a tent. So they take gear for wet and sunny weather.

When we are bereaved, we too have to be prepared. When we are busy thinking about what has happened to us, it means that for a little while, we might find concentrating at school more difficult or doing simple jobs harder, or we might even find ourselves clumsier and accident-prone. So we have to 'be prepared'. This means being kind to ourselves, not expecting too much and giving ourselves a little more time to do jobs at school or at home.

Are there any treats that you particularly like?

29
Christmas

Christmas is a time of holidays, fun, presents, food and a good time with your family. But it's also a time when you are more aware that the person who has died is no longer with you. Others in the family will also have mixed feelings. You might be excited about the presents, while another person in the family is feeling sad. You might be sad when others are having a good time. It's ok to be both happy and sad at the same time. Your loved one would want you to remember them but also to make the most of Christmas.

There are things you can do to help:

You can make a Christmas card for the person who has died and tell them about your Christmas. Why not make a present for them? It might be a picture, or sowing some seeds to make a plant for the spring. Making something helps you to think about the one who has died and it then allows you to focus on your Christmas time.

30
Holidays

Holidays are a time away from school to enjoy yourself with family and friends. Perhaps your family will go away somewhere special. But when someone has died, holidays can be difficult. It might be that your family do not feel up to going anywhere or just don't have the money to spend. This can be disappointing for you. Remember, your family can't help it; it will just take time for things to get back to some kind of normality. Holidays away without a special relative can feel strange for you and your family. But I'm sure the person who has died would want you to have a good time.

Before going away, why not visit the grave or a church and say a prayer to your loved one about what you are going to do? Writing a diary of your holiday and your thoughts can help.

31
Special times

After the death of someone, you eventually begin to have ordinary days of school, home, play, friends, food and sleep. The days can all blur together. You might still think about your loved one every day but there are many things to do that squeeze out your thoughts. Through the year there are special days to remember. The person's birthday and the anniversary day of when they died become special. It's a time to remember them in a deeper way than all the other days.

Buying a present for your loved one can give you something to do on the special day. It might be some flowers or a plant to put on the grave or leave in a special place. Special days are a good time to talk more to your relatives about the person who has died. Perhaps you still have questions to ask, or you would like to hear stories about them. Writing a letter to them can help you feel better. You could keep the letter or perhaps give it to a local vicar who could say a special prayer for you and light a candle for the person who has died.

32
A place to visit

If the person who has died has been buried, then visiting the grave can be a comfort to you. It's a chance to have a few minutes thinking and talking to your relative. Taking some flowers or tidying the grass gives you something you can do with your relatives or a friend. If the loved one has been cremated, then perhaps you could visit the place where the ashes were scattered. If they were killed in a road accident, perhaps a relative could take you to place some flowers near the accident spot. It can be helpful to take some flowers to the local church and have a few minutes sitting in the stillness and quietness of the church.

Have you got a special thinking place? Perhaps this is in the park, on the swings or somewhere in the garden. Use this place when you need a little time to yourself.

33
A memory box

When someone has died, we want to hold on to them for as long as possible. We can often be worried we might forget them. An easy way to help is to make a memory box. This is simply a shoebox that you can decorate and make special. Inside the box you can begin to collect things which remind you of the loved one. It might contain photographs, possessions, a favourite CD, the order of service leaflet from the funeral, or perhaps a pressed flower from the funeral. You can put the box somewhere safe and look at it when you want.

Can you get someone to help you with the box? How will you decorate it to make it special?

34
A memory jar

We all have our own personal memories of the one who has died. To make your memories special, make a memory jar which you can keep on the windowsill. You will need a small, long glass jar, some salt and some coloured chalk. Think of about five or six special memories of the person who has died and choose a colour that fits each memory. On some newspaper pour out a small amount of salt and rub it with the coloured chalk. When the salt becomes the colour you want, pour it into the jar. Do this with each colour/memory until the jar is full. The jar needs to be full to the brim before putting the lid on tight.

Before you begin, draw the jar and colour it the way you want it. Then mark each colour and write the memory next to it. This will help you not to forget. You can put this picture in your memory box. Make the memory jar with a relative and talk about the differences of each colour.

35
Press a flower

Did your special person have a favourite colour or a favourite flower? Perhaps they had a characteristic smell that you can still remember. It might be of some aftershave or perfume. Why not get a flower in their favourite colour and press it? Put it between two clean pieces of paper and then compress it in the middle of a heavy book. Eventually the flower will dry out. Put the flower between cellophane and keep it in your memory box.

Can you remember what flowers were used at the funeral? Perhaps you could get a similar flower to press.

36
Special music

Music helps us get in touch with our feelings. We all like different types of music to help us relax. Do you know what the person who died liked to listen to? Listening to their favourite music can help you to feel close to them. It can help you to bring back memories that you might have forgotten.

You will also have your own choice of music that you love. Use it to listen to when you feel unhappy or under pressure or just need to be by yourself.

If you are unsure what your loved one liked, then ask your relatives. You might be surprised!

37
Watching DVDs

Some families make DVDs of their holidays, Christmas times and general fun times. Other families use photographs as a way of capturing special times. When you watch a DVD or look at photographs of someone who has died, it can be very upsetting. But when you do this with other members of your family, it can also be very comforting. It helps you remember the one who has died, gives you a chance to talk, laugh and cry together, and can make you feel closer to your relatives.

Sometimes you or your relative won't feel like watching a DVD or looking at photographs. That is normal and ok. Choose a time when you both want to do it.

38
Being alone

After the funeral and when the relatives have all gone home, everyone tries to get on with their normal routine. Adults might go back to work, while you have to go to school. It's not long before no one seems to talk about the person who has died. Everyone seems busy and it can feel as if they hadn't existed. But you might find that you are thinking a lot about them. It can be a lonely time, with no one seeming to understand. This is very normal.

On good days keep busy and on difficult days be kind to yourself. Remember to use your first-aid kit to help you. When you feel very down, don't be afraid to talk to a relative, teacher or friend.

When you have a difficult day, are you better alone or with a friend?

39
The weather

Grief is like the weather, some days you get out of bed and the sun is shining and you feel fine. On other days you get up and it's cloudy and wet and you feel down. There seems to be no reason why you have good days and sad days, this is just how it is. We have little control of the weather or sometimes of our feelings. Remember, the weather gradually changes and so will your feelings. You just have to give it time. Before long you will find yourself moving from winter to spring and finally summer. Your grief, too, will change. In time it will gradually get easier.

What is your favourite season of the year? Draw a picture of the four seasons and on each write down your feelings.

40
Facing our fears

When someone has died, your mind begins to race. There are so many thoughts and questions. You might find that you can't stop thinking about the dead person. It's like a CD that's got stuck and keeps going round and round.

Some thoughts are about the past and how the person died. Other thoughts are about the present and how things are now at home and at school. Other thoughts are about the future and how it all affects you. It can help to write down your thoughts and questions. Then see if you can write down some possible answers.

Is there someone who could help you with the answers?

41
Guilt

Guilt is when you blame yourself for something that has gone wrong. We all feel guilty at different times in our life. But when someone dies, we can blame ourselves. This is a very natural feeling. We need to know that the death was not our fault. Children do not cause adults to die. If you are unsure, try to tell a relative how you feel and they can help to explain. If necessary ask to see a doctor and they can explain more fully why the person died.

You won't be the only person who may blame themselves. By talking to a relative you will be helping them as well as yourself.

42
Bubbles

When we are upset at the death of a person, we can feel guilty about many things. At school or at home there can be many things we can blame ourselves for. These guilt feelings are like air bubbles that we want to push deep under water. But the bubbles just keep floating to the surface. The only way to get rid of them is to burst the bubbles. We do this by talking to someone like a relative or teacher. They can help us see that all of these things are not our fault. It's just a sad feeling we get left with when someone has died. With reassurance these guilty feelings will go.

Can you draw a picture with lots of bubbles? Write in each bubble any guilty thoughts you might have.

43
Anger

Sometimes we can feel so angry inside that we want to shout and kick and we feel that we are about to burst like a balloon. There are many things to feel angry about when someone dies. We can be angry with ourselves, parents, grandparents, brothers or sisters, school, teachers, homework, friends, our pets, food, God, Jesus and even the person who has died.

Can you make a drawing of a volcano and write on the picture all the things that make you angry? Pin the picture on the wall. Make a paper aeroplane and colour it using what you think represents anger. Now throw it as hard as you can at your picture.

44
Letting rip

Children are not the only ones who can feel upset and angry. Adults can feel just as angry, but they are good at hiding their feelings, so you might not think they are angry. Some adults take their anger out on things and people. If an adult is taking their anger out on you, it's important you tell a responsible adult to help you. It's never right to take your anger out on another person or animal. Perhaps you find that you are taking your anger out on someone. There are better ways of dealing with it.

Ask a teacher to help you think about how you can control your anger.

45
Why?

One of the reasons we feel angry is that we can have questions that no one can answer. This might be the first time in our life when we have to face the fact that we can't get an answer. Sometimes as we get older we find different answers to our questions, but there are some questions we just can't find answers for. Even adults have questions that they can't answer. This doesn't mean we can't get on with learning, playing and making the most of our life.

Write down your questions in your diary or notebook. Over time you can keep on rethinking through possible answers.

46
Anger and love

Sometimes we get angry with the very people we love. We can feel angry with the person who has died because they have left us and are no longer with us. We can feel angry with those we live with because they are not the dead person who we want to be with. We can also be upset with them because they don't seem to be the same any more. It's ok to be angry with people. We can still love the people we are angry with.

What helps is to understand why people are the way they are. The loved one didn't want to leave you. They were either ill or had an accident. Even people who take their own lives must have been ill. Your family are perhaps behaving differently because they too are angry and upset and are having to adjust to the changes in their lives.

Remember, just because adults may not show any emotions, it doesn't mean that they are not feeling the same way you do. They just have a different way of dealing with it. Some adults don't want to show that they are upset because they don't want to upset you.

47
Don't panic

There's a comedy programme on TV called *Dad's Army* where an old soldier goes around shouting, 'Don't panic, don't panic!' But when someone has died we do feel like panicking. Your heart beats faster and it can feel as if you are carrying a huge parcel that you can't put down. What you need is others to help you carry your parcel. Remember your support circle (see **Friends who help**, page 15) and all your friends who are there to support you. The more we know there are others on our side at home or at school, the more we will feel calmer and able to cope with tomorrow.

When you feel in a panic, try to picture a very happy memory in your life. Try and recall all the good parts of the memory. How does it make you feel? Make a picture of it and put it on the wall to remind you of good times.

48
A plaster cast

Do you know somebody who has broken an arm or a leg? Usually the hospital puts what's called a plaster cast on the injured person. If they go to school, everyone knows that they have broken a bone. Sometimes they let their friends write and draw on the cast. After a few weeks the arm or leg mends and the cast is taken off.

When someone who is close to you dies, it's like breaking a leg or an arm. It hurts and takes time to get better. But you don't have a cast to remind everyone about your loss. So it's easy for them to forget your pain, but this doesn't mean it hurts any less.

Draw a picture of yourself with a cast on your arm or leg. On the cast write how you are feeling inside.

49
Draw a tree

Draw a big tree with many branches, filling the whole piece of paper. On the tree, draw lots of children. Some are climbing the tree. Others are sitting on a branch. One is reaching the very top of the tree and another has fallen off a branch. Another is being helped by a friend and one is sitting alone, crying. One is being pushed by someone and another child is sitting on the ground.

Colour the picture in. Now think about which child represents you.

How does it feel to be where you are on the tree? Would you like to be somewhere else? How do you think you can get there?

50 Falling

Sometimes we can feel like the child who has fallen out of the tree. We just don't have the energy to pick ourselves up and climb the tree again. We might not want to be in the picture at all and long to be with the person who has died. This is not a new experience. Over hundreds and hundreds of years, adults and children have had this experience. It's good to know that others have been where you are and have slowly got better. Many famous people in the past and present have experienced this pain. They all say the same thing – find someone to share your pain with. When you are ready, they can help you to begin to climb again.

Remember, you might not have a cast on your leg but you still need just as much support and help.

51
A cube

When you are sad or upset, people often ask, 'How are you feeling?' But often we just don't want to say anything. To help, you can make a cube out of a piece of card. Ask an adult to help you make the template. When it's made, colour one side red to represent an angry day. On each side use a different colour to represent a good day, a tired day, a leave-me-alone day, an I-want-to-talk day, and a sad day. Write on what each colour represents so that you don't forget. Use the cube each day or period of the day to show your family or friends how you are feeling.

Some days you might feel like all of the sides of the cube. Don't worry, that's very normal.

52
Looking for answers

When something big happens in our life, like someone dying, it raises many questions. These questions tend to pop up in our thoughts and then disappear again till another time. It can be good to write them down when you think of them because it's easy to forget them. There tend to be three types of questions. First there are questions about the past, secondly, questions about life now at home and at school and thirdly, questions about the future for you, your family and the person who has died.

See how many questions you can write down about the past, the present and the future.

53
Questions about the past

Questions about the past are often focused on the person who has died. These questions might be about their life and the things they did. We may want to know how they became ill or had an accident. Other questions will be about how they died and where they are now. See it as if you are doing a jigsaw of the person's life. As you get answers, you will be able to complete the picture of the past. Your family, the dead person's friends and the local doctor will be able to answer many of your questions.

Ask your relatives to let you see photographs of the dead person's life. There may also be a video that includes them.

54
Questions about the present

When someone in your home dies, it can change everyday life. The person who died might have done special tasks for you. Perhaps they did the cleaning or cooking in your house, or they were the one who always gave you a hug and played games with you. There may be someone else doing these tasks now, or perhaps no one does them. This can all seem very different and strange and leave you with lots of questions.

Is there someone at home or school you could talk to about how life is now different for you?

55
Questions about the future

Questions about the future don't all come at once. They seem to come bit by bit. New questions can keep coming to you long after the death of a person. Often we have very little questions which seem silly, so we don't want to ask them. But little questions can often be easily answered by adults. Sometimes adults find it harder to answer the bigger questions about the future because they have to adjust like you. Tomorrow is always a new day but some things won't change. Your family will still love and care for you, your teachers will always help you and you won't ever forget about the person who has died.

Can you draw a picture of what you would like the future to be like?

56
Finding answers

When you have lots of questions in your head, it can be hard to know who to ask to find the answers. Sometimes adults don't realise children are thinking these questions and so don't help them to find the answers. Some adults think by talking about the questions, you might get upset. They don't always realise that you are already upset inside your heart and mind. But when we get answers we are content with, it can help us to feel better and calmer and more able to think about other things.

You may think adults will have all the answers to your questions but often there will be questions that even the adults can't answer.

It can help by writing a letter to your relative, teacher or doctor and putting down your questions. Then, they can have time to think about it and find the best time to talk to you. Remember they might be asking the same questions as you.

57
Death

Death is something that happens to all plants, animals and human beings. Some plants and animals live for a very short time, just a day or a few weeks. Other plants and animals live for a very long time, like the great big trees or tortoises. It depends which country you live in, but many humans live for 70 to 85 years, although some die as babies and others live more than 100 years. Between birth and death, an accident or an illness can occur which ends a life.

Death is when the body stops working. It looks like sleep but it's very different. The body becomes still and never moves again. The heart and the mind stop working, the lungs stop breathing and the body gradually becomes cold. This body will never work again. It's like a toy that can't be fixed.

When someone dies, some children are given the chance to see the dead person. They usually just look as if they are sleeping, only much colder to touch and the skin is paler. If you didn't see your special person, ask a relative and they can tell you what they looked like.

58
Life after death

What happens to a person when they die? Because we haven't died ourselves, we don't know the answer to this fully, but people believe different things. Some believe that when a person dies, it's the end of their life. All that's left are the elements which remain after burial or cremation. Others believe that when you die, the body is left behind but the specialness of the person (called the spirit) goes to God and God gives the person a new, healthy body in a new, perfect world called heaven. We can't see heaven but it's where God lives. It's a place of wholeness and completeness. Religions believe different things about life after death. A school teacher could explain more fully.

What do you think happens when someone dies? Can you draw a picture of what you think?

59
Funerals

When a person is dead, we have to care for the body that is left. It's like the chrysalis that a butterfly leaves behind when it turns from a caterpillar to a butterfly. The chrysalis was important but now it's just an empty shell. The body is placed into a special box called a coffin and this is then taken to a special place, like a church or a chapel, where people come together for the funeral. This is a time to remember the dead person, give thanks for their life and to say goodbye.

Sometimes adults think children will get too upset to attend a funeral but normally children cope with it just like adults do.

Did you attend the funeral? If not, ask an adult who was there to tell you more about it. Can you draw a picture of what it was like?

60
Burial or cremation

After a funeral service the body is either cremated or buried. Bodies are buried in a church graveyard or in a cemetery. After the coffin is lowered into a hole and the grave is filled in with soil, people leave flowers and eventually get a gravestone made with the dead person's name on it. If the family decide to have the body cremated, the coffin is taken to a crematorium and after a very short service of prayers, the coffin is taken privately to a special oven where the coffin and body are burned. What is left behind is what we call the ashes. These can be buried or scattered in a special place.

Was your relative buried or cremated? Why not ask if you can take a few flowers to the grave or where the ashes were placed.

61
Are they really dead?

When we're told that someone has died, it can be very hard to believe it's true. At first we just can't believe it and won't believe it. Gradually, we realise that they are not around but might think that they will return. We can hope that they will be around for our birthday or for Christmas but when you are dead you can't come back for special occasions! Sometimes we dream about the dead person or think we see them in the street or hear or smell them. All of this makes us think they are around. Slowly these things fade and we are left with our memories of the dead person.

Have you ever shouted in a valley or near rocks and heard an echo coming back to you? Gradually the echo fades. This is what it's like when someone dies. Their presence gradually fades from you.

62
Heaven

Christians believe that heaven is a special place where God makes people whole and complete. Because we haven't been to heaven, we struggle to know much about it. Sometimes people say it's in the sky or it's like the stars. What we mean is that it's out of reach to us. But the Bible does tell us that heaven is like a big mansion or house that God has made, where he will take care of us. It's a place where there is no more illness or suffering or death. God makes wonderful things. Some of them we see on earth, like the plants and animals. Would God have made special things for heaven?

Can you paint a picture of what you think heaven is like?

63
Will we meet again?

This is a question that everyone asks. Some people don't think we will ever see our loved ones again but other people are very certain that they will meet again. Christians believe that a loving God would want us to be reunited with those we care for. This means that we would recognise them with their new bodies. But God also tells us to make heaven on earth in the meantime by doing our best and making earth a caring place. There will be a time to meet our loved one, but now is the time to grow, learn and care for our families who need our support.

Write a letter to the person who has died, telling them all the things you are doing in your life.

64
Enjoy without forgetting

Losing someone you have loved is a very big thing to adjust to. It all seems so negative and painful. In time you can choose to make this more positive by taking your loved one with you in your thoughts into the rest of your life. Doing new things is a way of giving thanks for the person who has died. They would want you to make the most of your life. Sometimes people carry something small to remember the person who has died. Make sure it isn't too precious or valuable, in case you lose it.

Get a dice and throw it a few times. Add the numbers up and whatever number it comes to, think about what you might be doing when you are that age.

65
Learn something new

Can you remember when you learned to ride a bicycle? Although at first it's a scary feeling, when you have learned to balance by yourself it can feel very exciting and rewarding. Learning new activities can be a good way of helping yourself to recover from your loss. It won't bring back the dead person but it will help you to begin to adjust to your new life.

Is there a friend that you could learn something new with? Your school might run after-school activities that you could join. You don't have to be good at something, just willing to have a go.

66
No one is looking

When someone close to you has died, it's easy to lose your confidence and not want to leave your home. Going to school and playing out with friends can seem very hard work. It can feel as if you are wearing an extra layer of skin. Other people might not be aware of it, but you know that you wear it everywhere. The good news is that although you feel different, you do not look different. People are not looking at you as much as you might think. When you first go back to school, people might make a comment to you but they soon forget and busy themselves with other matters. They quickly forget you have had a loss and at times you might wish that they did remember.

Being confident is like something that is given to you. It never comes in lorry loads but always in little envelopes. If you do little things each day, you will find your confidence grows.

67
Hiccups

Have you ever had hiccups? They come suddenly and are hard to control. Then they seem to stop but come back when you don't expect them. When you are recovering from the death of someone, it can feel as if you have hiccups. You start to feel better and then you have a bad day. Then you get your confidence again and you begin to do well, only to find that along comes another bad day. Don't worry, this is just how it is. Slowly the bad days get fewer, until you forget about them.

Can you remember the last time you had hiccups? How did you try to get rid of them? Remember, they did go in the end.

68
Standing on the seashore

Have you ever been to the seaside and had a walk along the beach? You can walk along the edge of the dry sand away from the water, only to find that a big wave comes in and catches your feet. You walk a little further and again the wave catches you. Thinking about the dead person is like this. You have times when you don't think about them at all and then suddenly a thought comes to you. You then get on with playing games and going to school until another thought hits you. Just as the sea is meant to go in and out with the tide, this is how you react when a person dies.

Draw a picture of the seaside with the waves coming and going. Is the tide in or out?

69
Friends

Have you got a special friend or friends? When someone dies, friends often don't know what to say or do. Perhaps you have had a friend who has been upset about something. Did you know what to do? Friends don't know whether to visit you or not. Whether to talk about the dead person or not. To help you at school or leave you alone. And often you don't know what you want them to do. Just as you are adjusting to change, they are adjusting to you feeling upset. We have to be forgiving to our friends when they don't understand how we feel or what we want. But sometimes we have to find new friends who will help us better.

It's ok to want to be alone or to want to be with friends. If you don't want to play with your friends, just tell them you'll play another time when you feel like it.

70
Wishing dead

When you get hurt by someone, it can make you feel so angry that it's easy to think or say you wish the person dead. Just for a split second you might really wish it. It might be to a parent or brother or sister or step-relative. Later, if that person dies, you might feel as if it was your fault. You might think it was what you said, thought or did that caused the death.

Everyone gets so angry at times that we can think bad thoughts about another person. But it's never the reason why the person died. People don't die because of our thoughts or words.

If you are unsure, ask a relative why the person died and share with them what you have been thinking. They will help you understand the true reason why the person died.

71
No replacement

When someone dies in a family, it leaves a gap. Sometimes another person comes and does the jobs that the dead person would have done. This might make you feel upset and angry. It can make you feel as if people are quickly forgetting the dead person and trying to replace them. But everyone is unique and special, so no one can replace the person who has died. That doesn't mean your family doesn't need help and support from another person. Your dad or mum might need help from another adult as they cope with their loss. As much as children can help, and this is very important and appreciated, adults still need help from other adults.

Does it feel as if someone is trying to push into your family? Is there someone at school you could talk to about this? Remember, no one can replace your loved one, but we do need others to come and help us.

72
Forgiving others

Have you ever been on your bike when someone has pushed you off? It can make you feel very angry with them. When people hurt you, it can be difficult to forgive them. It might be the person who has died, or the people you live with, or someone at school. When we don't forgive, we are not hurting the other person but ourselves. It's not easy to forgive someone. This is because we are still angry with them. If we can't forgive them all at once, perhaps we can forgive them bit by bit. The more you are able to forgive, the more you will be able to help yourself.

When you forgive someone, it doesn't mean that you allow them to go on hurting you. Can you think of times when someone has forgiven you?

73
Forgiving oneself

When things go wrong, it's natural to blame ourselves. We can blame ourselves for many things – for the death of the person, because adults around us are not coping, because life isn't the same, because our school work is poor, or many other things. We might feel we need to be punished and start to hurt ourself. Although this might make us feel better at first, it doesn't remove the feeling or the problem. In fact, it only makes things worse.

We have to deal with two things: first, who is really to blame? Secondly, we have to deal with the feelings inside of us.

Is there something you blame yourself for? Do you ever hurt yourself? Can you draw a picture of this?

74
Who is to blame?

Who is to blame when somebody dies? Sometimes there is no one to blame, it's just how the world is. Accidents happen and people become ill for no reason. The world is not perfect so it means that people make mistakes and things break. But usually no one wants another person to die, even if they were involved in the accident. Hospitals and doctors try their best to help, but they can't cure all illnesses. When someone dies we naturally feel angry. This anger is usually directed at someone or something. So we blame the doctor, the hospital, the person who was involved in the accident, ourselves, our family or God. But most of the time it's no one's fault, not even yours.

Have you ever blamed someone for the death? How do they feel about the death?

75
Expressing feelings

When someone dies we have a mixture of feelings. We feel hurt or pain inside us. We feel angry at what has happened. We feel guilty even though it wasn't our fault. We feel fearful that someone else will die and we just feel all anxious inside as if there were butterflies in our stomach. All of these feelings are no good inside us; they need to be let out slowly and carefully.

We let out our hurt by talking to someone who will listen. Our anger needs to be got rid of in a safe way that doesn't hurt anyone else (see **Anger**, page 48). We deal with fear by being reassured by other people that everything is going to be ok. And only then do those butterflies start to disappear.

Can you draw a bin and put into it all the feelings you have inside you?

76
If only . . .

Have you got a favourite song or CD that you like playing? We can listen to the same song over and over again. We can do this with thoughts in our head. We can keep thinking the same thing constantly. Perhaps it's, 'If only things were different.' There can be many 'if only's'. If only they hadn't died, if only they could come back, if only it hadn't happened, if only I could see them again. All the 'if only's' can't change anything. You have to change the record and begin to think different thoughts.

Can you write down all your 'if only's' and replace them with new sentences that begin, 'I'm thankful for . . . '?

77
A long journey

Have you ever been on a country walk or a long bike ride? It can seem to go on for ever. You just think you are getting to the end of your journey when there is another hill to climb. But eventually you do arrive at your destination. It's like this when someone you care about dies. You have good days, then sad days and then ordinary days, only to be followed by another sad day. But as you journey, each day you are learning, getting stronger and wiser. It's only as you look back that you can see how far you have travelled.

Each day in your diary or notebook draw a picture of what kind of day it has been.

78
Getting taller

Each day you are in a process of growing, getting taller and changing in your appearance. This is true for all young people. We are also changed by the things that happen to us in life. Home, school, people, and the things that happen to us all affect us, making us a unique individual.

The death of someone can also change us. But we can choose to either make the change for the better or the worse. We can choose to become thankful that we have known the person who died. We can choose to be caring to our family members and understand others at school who also have losses in their lives.

Measure yourself against a wall and keep checking it every week.

79
Paint a picture

Have you ever been to an art gallery and looked at the paintings? If not, look at the paintings on the walls of your school. If you get close up to an oil painting, you will see that it looks very messy. But as you stand back and look at the picture, it all becomes very clear. We can feel like this when we are grieving. Each day, you don't think things are getting better. But it's only later, as you look back at all that you have come through and learned, that you can see more clearly.

Paint a picture of how you see your life today. Do this again in four weeks' time. Keep doing it each month and see how the pictures change.

80
Being special

Just as the person who has died was special, you also are very special. In the Bible there is a prayer that King David says. It's called Psalm 139. In this prayer it tells of how God knew you even before you were born. He knew you in your mother's womb and was with you when you were born. King David also says that everyone is unique, special and wonderfully made. This is you. There is no one else in the world who looks, thinks or behaves exactly like you. No one else can live your life, only you. It's up to you now to make the most of your life. King David asked God to help him live his life right, using his gifts and abilities and being kind to others.

Look in a mirror and say to yourself, 'I am wonderfully made, I am special.' You are special, whether you feel like it or not.

81
Where is God?

When we think of God, we can think he is like Superman or Batman who can zoom in and stop bad things from happening. But if God did this, he would be always interfering in our lives. Remember when you learned to ride a bike, your parents had to let you try by yourself. Sometimes you would fall off your bike before you finally learned. Your parents, even though they were with you, had to take a risk that you might fall and have a bad injury. Although sad things happen and God doesn't want these things to happen, it's also part of how we learn and grow.

Draw a picture of a tree with deep roots. Let the roots represent God. The trunk represents your life so far (with scars) and the branches represent all your hopes for the future. Notice we don't always see the roots but they are there, supporting the tree.

82
Who is God?

The Bible has lots of different names for God to help us understand him. He is called:

- **the holy one**, which means he is perfect and special.
- **the light**, the one who helps us to see the way ahead.
- **the comforter**, the one who wants to support us at difficult times.
- **the way, the truth and the life**, which means he wants to help us face the truth of what has happened to us, help us to recover and to make the most of our life.
- **the beginning and the end** (the alpha and omega), which means he knows us at the beginning of our life, throughout our life and wants to make all things whole and complete at the end.

Can you draw a picture of what God is like for you?

83
How can God help me?

Many people find help and strength by believing in God, especially at difficult times. They say or think prayers to him. Prayers are a way of talking to God about all the things in our life. They read stories about him in the Bible of how he helped other people. They believe that he is with them in their life and has promised to never leave them. They get encouraged because God wants them to make the most of their life, their time and ability. They believe he is taking care of the person who has died and will one day bring them all together. When we believe that God is on our side, it can strengthen us through difficult and lonely times.

Do you know of any stories in the Bible when God helped someone? You could ask to speak to your local vicar who works in the church and comes into your school, to help you understand God better.

84
Feeling alone

Many people have found this poem helpful when they have been feeling alone and that God is far from them. It's called 'Footprints'.

One night I dreamed I was walking
along the beach with the Lord.
Many scenes from my life flashed across the sky.
In each scene I noticed footprints in the sand.
Sometimes there were two sets of footprints,
other times there was one set of footprints.

This bothered me because I noticed
that during the low periods of my life,
when I was suffering from anguish, sorrow or defeat,
I could see only one set of footprints.

So I said to the Lord,
'You promised me Lord, that if I followed you,
you would walk with me always.
But I have noticed that during the most trying periods
of my life there have only been one set
of footprints in the sand.
Why, when I needed you most,
have you not been there for me?'

The Lord replied,
'The times when you have seen only one set of
footprints in the sand, is when I carried you.'

Mary Stevenson 1922-1999

85
Prayer

You can pray at any time, day or night. Prayer is just chatting to God about the things in your life that concern you. Most people pray when they wake up or when they go to bed at the end of the day. But you can also pray in the car, at school or even on the toilet! You don't have to say the prayer out loud. God will hear you as you say it in your thoughts. You can tell God about the good things and the difficult things that have happened to you in the day. You can ask him to take care of your loved ones, including the person who has died. You can ask him to strengthen you to cope with each day. God is like the bridge between you and your loved one; he keeps you connected with each other.

Why not write your prayers out in your diary or notebook and then keep them in your memory box?

86
Talking to the loved one

It's very normal to still want to talk to the person who has died. It can be comforting to think that they still hear you. At the end of the day is a good time to think about your loved one and to share your day with them. Writing letters in your notebook can also help. Thinking that your loved one hears you and is supporting you can help to give you confidence to deal with new challenges at school and at home. You might be able to think about what words of wisdom the loved one would want to say to you.

What things would you like to say to the person who has died?

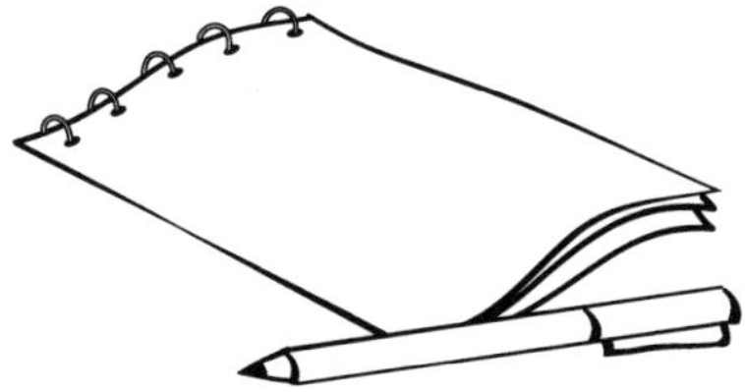

87
When Jesus died

Christians believe that Jesus was God's Son and that he came to earth to show us how to live. He allowed himself to die to show us how much God cares for us and suffers with us in our suffering. When he was dying, Jesus told another man on the cross that when they died they would be in paradise, another word for heaven.

After Jesus died and before he went to heaven, Jesus appeared to many people. He did this to show us that he could overcome death and give us hope for our loved ones and ourselves. Jesus said he would be with us in heaven to make all things well. But he also promised to be with us on earth. He said he would send his Spirit (like an invisible cloak) to comfort us and to guide us. When we pray, it's Jesus' Spirit that is with us, helping us.

By believing in Jesus, the disciples (his friends) found new strength and hope for their future.

88
Special Bible readings

Have you got a special story that you like reading over and over? The Bible is a very big book but there are special parts that people find helpful to read over and over again. Here are just a few:

When afraid:
Mark 4:35-41

When upset:
1 Corinthians 15:51-57
1 Thessalonians 4:13-18
Revelation 21:3-5

When thinking about death:
John 3:16
John 14:1-3

When feeling lost:
Luke 19:10
Ephesians 2:12, 13
Psalm 107:4-9

When friends fail:
2 Timothy 4:16-18

When lonely:
Revelation 3:20
Psalm 23

When needing peace:
John 14:27

When praying:
1 John 5:14, 15
Luke 11:1-13

When worried:
Matthew 6:25-34
Philippians 4:6, 7

When tired:
Matthew 11:28-30
2 Corinthians 4:16-18
Psalm 116:4-7

At the front of a Gideon Bible you will find a list of favourite readings to help you at special times. Your school might have a Gideon Bible; if not ask a relative to get in touch with the Gideons and they will give you a free Bible.

89
Church

Church is a special place to focus on God and to be with other people who want to find his support. Most churches have children's and youth groups where young people have fun together. But it's also a place where the old and young try and put into practice what Jesus taught about loving and caring for people. This could be a place where you find other young people of your age who will understand you and want to support you. Church is also a place where we learn more about God, about how to pray and understand the Bible and how to find God's support at difficult times.

Is there someone at school you could talk to about finding a church near you? Is there someone at school who comes to lead assemblies that you enjoy?

90
Extra help

However supportive your family, school or church might be, there are times when we all need extra help. Sometimes it can be good to meet other people of your own age who have had a similar experience. Wherever you live, there may be a child bereavement charity near you that can offer one-to-one support or a chance to join a small group of young people.

See page 106 for support groups contacts.

Support groups have lots of fun together. At first it can feel strange but as you make friends, you will see how supportive you can be to each other.

91
Suicide

Suicide is when someone takes their own life. It's like an illness of the mind in which they are not thinking about anything else but ending their life. It's not that they don't love you or care for you; they have just become trapped in how they are thinking. We can be left with lots of questions, some of which we can't ever answer. What's very important is to know that it was not your fault and you mustn't blame yourself. Also, that it doesn't mean you will take your life one day. You don't have to tell people that your loved one committed suicide if you don't want to. You can decide to just say, 'They died in tragic circumstances.'

Just as the person chose to end their life, you can choose to learn from it by making the most of your life. If you feel angry with the person who has died, write them a letter to express your feelings. Keep it in your memory box.

Remember, always ask for help if you feel life is difficult. When we share our problems, it makes them seem smaller.

92
Murder

When someone close to us is murdered, it's a very big shock. You will feel very angry with the murderer and perhaps with your family for allowing it to happen. You will have lots of questions going around in your head:

Why did it happen?
Why didn't the murderer kill someone else?
Why didn't my relative escape?
Why couldn't I stop it?
Why don't the police catch the person?
Why are the TV stations and newspapers interested?
Why don't they all leave us alone?

If the police accuse someone in your family, you will feel even more confused.

Your family will all be under a lot of pressure and may find themselves arguing. You will need lots of support in the months ahead.

Ask your relatives or school to find a counsellor or friend who can support you over a long period. This person can help you work through the questions you have. It will take time to adjust to the change but gradually, with support, you can overcome this tragedy.

Keeping a diary each day will help you to express your feelings and keep track of what is happening to you.

93
Death of a mother or father

When a mum or dad dies, it leaves a big gap in your life and in your family. Everyone in the family has to make changes. The parent who is alive will have to work harder to keep the family together. It will mean that they will not only be missing their partner and feeling upset, but will also be a lot more tired from all the extra work. It might feel as if your living parent isn't the same any more. Your brothers and sisters will also be trying to adjust to the change. It can mean that there may be more arguments.

Parents often hide their crying and don't show that they are upset. They are just trying to protect you, but it doesn't mean that they didn't care for the dead person. Just as it will take time for you to adjust to the change, so it will for your family members. Make sure you always find a space for yourself where you can be away from any pressure.

Remember, no one expects you to replace your mum or dad or try and do all the jobs that they did in the house. One day you will be an adult who your parents would be proud of, but until then try and enjoy just being your age and doing all the things you used to do.

Still make a Father's or Mother's Day card to remind you that you still have parents, even though one of them is not with you.

94
Death of a brother or sister

When a brother or sister dies, you can have very mixed feelings. Perhaps the brother or sister was older than you and you spent a lot of time arguing or fighting. You might have said you wished them dead. Or they might have been younger and got more attention from your parents. This is especially true if your brother or sister had been ill for a long time in hospital. Whether you resented your brother or sister or said nasty things to them, their death was not your fault. Everyone falls out with brothers and sisters, that's just how it is, but people don't die because of it. When you remember your brother or sister, remember them as they really were with their good points and their bad points.

You can't replace your brother or sister but you can be yourself with your own abilities and interests.

95
A changed family

When your parent dies, your mother or father may find it hard to be without their partner. Months or years later, they may find someone else to live with. This person may have children of their own. This will mean a big change for you. The new person can never replace your mum or dad and it's easy to resent them coming into your home. It doesn't mean that your parent has stopped loving your dead mother or father or loves you any less. It just means that they need another adult to support them. It's easy to take your anger out on the new partner as a way of punishing your mum or dad. But it will only make things worse.

Try and be thankful for all the good times you have had with your parents. See it like the end of a chapter in a book. In this new chapter, see if you can still have good times and accept that the new adult is just different from your dead mum or dad.

Can you talk to a grandparent, uncle, aunt or teacher about how things are changing at home?

96
When the dead person hurt you

Not everyone feels sad when someone dies. If the person has hurt you and been cruel to you, then you might be glad that they have died. Everyone is expecting you to be upset but inside you are pleased that they are dead. You might feel both pleased and sad all at once. When people have hurt you, you have a right to be angry and pleased that they are now not able to hurt you any more. No one should hurt another person, it's always wrong to do so.

However, you might feel guilty for feeling like this. This can all be very confusing. It's like two balls of wool tangled up together. You will need help from a counsellor or teacher to help you sort out your feelings.

Remember that although you may be relieved that the person can't hurt you any more, others may be very upset that he or she has died.

Have you told anyone that this person used to hurt you? It's important that you tell someone, like a teacher, so that you get the right support.

97
A special letter

It can be very helpful to write a letter to the person who has died. Although you can't post it, the letter allows you to say some important things. When you have written it, you can put it in your memory box, or give it to the local vicar to offer it to God, or perhaps you just want to show it to a relative.

The letter should first say thank you to the person for letting you get to know them. Secondly, you can share a special memory or memories you have, when you both did something together. Thirdly, share something that you are sorry about or that you regret and ask them for forgiveness. Fourthly, tell them that you forgive them for anything that they might have done to you that you didn't like. Finally, tell them it has been good to know them and it's now time for you to say goodbye. Sign your letter, place it in an envelope and put it somewhere safe.

Why not draw a picture with your letter of a special time you had together?

98
When you are no longer bereaved

Have you been on a car journey with your family that seems to go on and on? It seems as if you will never arrive at your holiday destination. Perhaps you or a brother or sister kept saying, 'Are we there yet?' But eventually, you do arrive and can begin to explore and enjoy your holiday.

When you have had a close relative die, it can seem as if your life never gets back to how it was before the death. A person has died and they won't be coming back. The journey that you have been on seems to have had many ups and downs to overcome and the road never seems to end. But when you look back, you will see you have come through many obstacles and are a stronger person because of it. There will be a time when you still remember the dead person, but it doesn't hurt so much. You reach a point when you can now enjoy your life, carrying your loved one with you in your thoughts and heart, taking with you all the things you have learned.

Look through your memory box and diary and see how far you have travelled. Perhaps you would like to redo your road-map and put on it all the new things you have learned and done.

99
Lessons learned

I hope you now realise that your special relative has not been left behind on your journey. They have journeyed with you, shaping and influencing you. At first they filled all your thoughts, but now it's as if you are carrying a small, precious jewel that contains all your special memories. A part of them will always be with you.

You have changed and grown on this journey. You have worked through your memories, feelings and hopes for the future. You have overcome times when you were very moody. Although at times it felt as if you were going backwards, and you were all alone, you have moved forwards and onwards. Congratulate yourself on your achievement.

Are there any lessons you have learned that could help other people? Don't be surprised if you need to read some of these pages over and over again on your journey.

100
A ship's journey

Once upon a time, people stood and watched a ship sail out of the harbour. They said goodbye as the ship disappeared over the horizon, leaving them all behind. But just as the ship disappeared, others saw the ship coming over the horizon and said hello and welcomed the ship home. This is how it is for those who die. But it's also like this for those left behind.

Your life is like a ship that is heading on a journey. You can't stay in the harbour and keep everything as it is. Life forces you out onto the sea for an adventure. We don't know what the journey will be like but you will probably have some good and bad weather. Family and friends will travel with you and God has promised to be with you, even in the heaviest of storms. I hope you become a great sailor of life and from your experiences help many other people along the way.

Can you imagine yourself on a ship, looking backwards with all your memories and looking forward to hope to come? Draw a final picture of this scene for your memory box and then place the box somewhere safe.

101
Find support

England
Child Bereavement Network
Tel. 020 7843 6309
www.ncb.org.uk

Buckinghamshire
Child Bereavement Charity
Tel. 01494 446648
www.childbereavement.org.uk

Cambridgeshire
Stars
Tel. 01223 815124
www.talktostars.com

Dorset
Counselling Care (Bill Merrington)
Tel. 07894 598915
www.counsellingcare.org

Gloucestershire
Winston's Wish
Tel. 0845 2030405
www.winstonswish.org.uk

Lancashire
RD4Uat Cruse
Tel. 0808 808 1677
www.rd4u.org.uk

London
The Candle Trust
Tel. 020 8768 4586
www.stchristophers.org.uk

Grief Encounter
Tel. 020 8446 7452
www.griefencounter.com

Kites Bereavement Service
Tel. 020 8525 6000
www.stjh.org.uk

Manchester
Manchester Area Bereavement Forum
Tel. 0161 371 8860
www.mabf.org.uk

Midlands East
Relate (Coventry)
Tel. 0845 130 4010
www.relate.org.uk

Midlands West
Edward's Trust
Tel. 0121 456 4838
www.edwardstrust.org.uk

North East
Sunderland Children and Young People
Counselling Service
Tel. 0191 553 5206
www.sunderlandcounselling.org.uk

Oxfordshire
Face2Face
Tel. 01993 892424
www.spired.com

Seesaw
Tel. 01865 744768
www.seesaw.org.uk

Yorkshire
Forget Me Not
Tel. 01642 296912
www.teessidehospice.org/childrens-bereavement

If you would like to share your thoughts, you can write to me (Bill Merrington) at ***support@counsellingcare.org***

Helping children – advice to adults

Whether you are a parent, teacher or supporter, you can play an important role in helping children adjust to the loss of a close relative or friend. Below is a list of guidance points which should give you confidence to support and stay with the child as long as it takes.

- Look after yourself and find support to help you handle your concerns. Children suffer not only the death of a loved one but also the loss of a parent in grief. The more you care for yourself, the more you will help your child.

- Children model their behaviour on your behaviour and coping skills. If they can't see or understand your grief it will make them think you don't care, increase their guilt and might leave them feeling worse.

- Avoid changes that are not necessary in the child's life. The more stable the home and school life, the easier it will be for the child to adjust.

- Don't force children into situations that are stressful. We need to listen to them to find out what is stressful or fearful for them. Only then can we begin to help them to work through an answer.

- Don't make decisions for them; allow them to express their views and opinions, even if you have to ultimately make the decision.

- By sharing your feelings with a child you are helping them to understand their feelings and to normalise their experience.

- Help the child to express their feelings in a positive way through talking, sport, play, music and artwork.

- Don't assume that the child does not want to talk just because they are silent. They need opportunities and encouragement to share their feelings and ask questions.

- Expect that the child will oscillate with their emotions, sometimes appearing fine and at other times very upset. This is normal.

- Be ready for the child to have increased anxiety, fears and to be more clingy than normal. Insecurity can lead to increased hyperactivity and behavioural problems. The child will need a clear structure and consistency to enable them to feel secure.

- Children often regress in their learning for a period after a loss. Compensate with more support and encouragement. They may need specialist help if it continues.

- Children need good communication about what has happened. They need to be assured about the future and made aware of any changes that might take place in the future.

- Children cope with hospitals, doctors and funerals. They deal with these places and events in a way according to their age. The more we protect them from such experiences, the more we are preventing them from making sense of what has happened to them.

- Bereaved children who are given the facts and appropriate support develop a coping mechanism that enables them to handle losses later in life.

- Remember there are appropriate books, aids and support groups available to offer help. Take all the support you can get.